Get Unstuck

Now!

Get Unstuck Now!

The Simple Guide to Restart Your Life

John Seeley M.A.

Heart Fire Press
San Diego, CA USA

Get Unstuck Now! The Simple Guide to Restart your Life

© 2023, 2014, 2005 John Herbert Seeley
Based on the workshop, Get Unstuck! © 2003 by John Herbert Seeley
Published by Heart Fire Press
EDITORIAL OFFICE
Heart Fire Press
4630 Border Village Road Suite 283
San Diego, CA
U.S.A.

Library of Congress Cataloging-in-Publication Data
Seeley, John Herbert
Get Unstuck Now! The Simple Guide to Restart Your Life / John Herbert Seeley M.A.
p. cm. Based on the workshop "Get Unstuck" © 2003, 2005, 2014, 2023

Editorial and production: Bob Adams
Cover design: Farah Evers
Cover photo: Larry Silva © 2023
ISBN 978-1-945533-12-9
Originally published as ISBN 0-595-29337-9, ISBN 0-976-5942-0-X
Printed in the USA on acid-free paper
Distributed by Heart Fire Press

This book is dedicated to my mom, Margaret Seeley, who always believed in me.

Contents

Introduction

Having been stuck several times in my life, I wanted to find out how to break free, move in the direction I wanted, and create the life I yearned for. I studied and searched for answers from many sources. I have written this book as a simple guide for you to refer to when you feel stuck in any part of your life.

Ask yourself if any of this applies to you.

Sometimes you feel you're in a place where you never planned to be. You aren't sure why you're there. You don't know exactly how you got there. You're often not even sure where you really want to be. Even if you do know where you would rather be, it's likely you aren't exactly sure how to get there.

This book is meant to help give you a new perspective and the tools to create the life you really desire!

Get Unstuck! is intended to be a guide to help you find your own answers to what you really want. It begins with the understanding of the process of changing your life. It provides an understanding of the process, beginning with accepting where you are, recognizing there is a way out, and being open to the possibility of miracles.

Understanding how you either grow or decay gives motivation for you to choose to grow again. The power of your word and its ability to create your wishes and dreams are explored. Realizing the motivation of humans as being either fear or desire, allows you to take a look at how your life has been created, and choose which you want to create your future.

Anger, being neither good nor bad, is offered to explain the exchange of energy that goes on in every relationship. This subconscious energy explanation is the key to understanding many of our misunderstandings in life. Examining criticism and encouragement helps to give you guidance toward achieving the desired outcomes in life.

The ability to change your mind, and use the tools to take back your power, is explained, in order to help you break down the walls that have kept you from realizing your dreams. Forgiveness and its powerful life-changing benefits are carefully detailed to allow you to understand how to break free from past issues and move forward again.

Developing your connection to your subconscious mind allows you to remove mental blocks, and create amazing results that you never thought possible.

Not only is the power of your commitment explained, it is also unequivocally solicited to ensure that you put the wisdom gained from this book into practice. Gratitude is also shown to be another tool for creating more of what you want out of life. Gratitude puts you in a place of having and not a place of "lack." Living life in a place of "lack" is often the result of feeling stuck. Finally, this book gives you specific, action-oriented steps to move forward and create a plan to help you advance from a place of feeling stuck, into a place of creative action.

Take this opportunity to do something for yourself. Read this book through completely once, then read it again and this time answer the questions after you finish each chapter. It is sometimes challenging to look at what has held you back in your life. Use this as a chance to rediscover your dreams again. I hope it will guide you to break free and create the life you always wanted!

1

Changing Your Life

*"To continue doing the same thing
and expecting different results is
insanity."*

–Albert Einstein

Change happens instantly! Deciding to change usually takes some time—sometimes years. When your life isn't going the way you want or expect, it's time to change. People change all the time; sometimes it's for the better, sometimes not. Often we resist change because what we have now is familiar and comfortable. It may not be exactly what you want, but it's not the worst thing in the world. You may want to change, but you don't know how. Maybe you just feel stuck in a rut. When you reach a place of frustration and hopelessness regarding a problem; that's the time to reach out for help. Perhaps you just need reinforcement. Asking for help for some people represents failure.

Do you tell yourself, "I couldn't do it on my own, so I'm a failure?" On the other hand, maybe you say, "If I have to ask for help, there must be something wrong with me."

The truth is, asking for help is many times the best thing you can do. The problem is, sometimes you might feel like you don't deserve help or, worse yet, there is no chance of helping you. That's when you have to reach out. There's always help, and once in a while you're just too close to the picture to see it. Sometimes you "think" you can see your situation accurately, and you conclude that there is no way you can be helped, but your conclusion is wrong. No matter what, there's help!

One of the keys to understand is knowing that you matter. As long as you believe you matter, you will find a way out. I'm speaking from experience in this area. I had been diagnosed as "clinically depressed." I wasn't locked up in a "loony bin," but I definitely needed professional help. My story is like many other people. In my case, it started with what I had called my "worst year." I was fired twice in six months. That was quite a shock to me. I had never been fired before, much less twice! I didn't know that in the restaurant field, there is a lot of turnover as part of the normal business cycle. I could have taken this as a signal that maybe I should look at another career. I wish I had! Instead, I read my firings as a message that I must not be "good enough."

I did not expect what came next. My best friend committed suicide, and I was the one who found him. This really tipped my world upside down. Shortly thereafter, my dog died. What more could happen? I became so depressed that I was very defensive with the people around me. I was very angry and frustrated. I felt helpless. Worse, I didn't know why all this was happening. I lashed out verbally when I felt I was being attacked, even when no one was attacking me! Because of this, I lost my fiancé. I took another job in the hope of saving the relationship, not to mention to help my self-esteem. Again, due to my defensiveness, I lost that too. This was another validation that I was a "loser."

Years later, I was still in denial about the reality of my life pattern. In fact, I used to tell my sad story to others to cheer them up. They would think, "Well, my life isn't as bad as his." I used this as proof that I was a martyr, as well. Therefore, I got sympathy from people.

In reality, I was a victim, and victimhood is not a good thing. It disempowers you. You think you're doing the best that you can, but being a victim just prolongs your suffering. At that time in my life, I felt I had no part of the situation, other than being on the receiving end of a dump truck filled with crap.

What I didn't realize then, was what happened in my outside world was a reflection of what I felt on the inside, and I was afraid to look at it. Often times when you find yourself in a depressed state, you get to a place of forgetting that you matter.

The logic sometimes goes like this, "I'm in such a bad place, I must deserve this. There's no hope, since I can't see any solutions. If there were a way out, I would see it. If I mattered, I wouldn't be in a position like this one. Like Jimmy Stewart in *It's a Wonderful Life*, we tell ourselves, "The world would be better off if I never lived." However, like in the movie, we don't realize how many people we touch every day in our lives. Some small thing we do today might save someone's life tomorrow. You don't have to believe in fate to know we all affect one another.

Sometimes just a smile, or kind word to a stranger, can pass on positive effects to many people. In *It's a Wonderful Life*, Jimmy meets an angel that helps him realize his life matters to many people. We may not all be visited by an angel-in-training who helps us see more clearly, but we have family, friends, strangers, therapists, television shows, books, etc., that help us become self-aware. In fact, we have an endless variety of resources to point our way to hope. Hope is our way out. We just have to see the message.

Knowing we deserve to find our way out is the first step. The fact that you're reading this book shows you are moving forward. So, keep reading and be open to creating positive results in your life.

Intention is powerful. You have to get clear on your intention to achieve the results you want. Like the book, *The 7 Habits of Highly Effective People*, you have to "begin with the end in mind." Knowing where you want to end up is essential, and knowing where you are is the first step to planning your path to get there. If you believe it's possible, you can find your way there.

"This guy's walking down the street when he falls in a hole. The walls are so steep he can't get out. A doctor passes by and the guy shouts up, 'Hey you. Can you help me out?'" The doctor writes a prescription, throws it down in the hole, and moves on. "Then a priest comes along, and the guy shouts up, 'Father, I'm down in this hole can you help me out?'" The priest writes out a prayer, throws it down in the hole, and moves on. "Then a friend walks by, 'Hey, Joe, it's me, can you help me out?'" And the friend jumps in the hole. Our guy says, 'Are you stupid? Now we're both down here.'" The friend says, "Yeah, but I've been down here before, and I know the way out."

–The West Wing

Useful questions:

- ❖ What do I want more of in my life?

- ❖ How do I affect others, both positively and negatively?

- ❖ How do I want my life to change?

- ❖ What are some small ways I can make a change?

Notes

Notes

"Get up. Stand up.
Stand up for your life!"

—Bob Marley

2

There is a Way Out

"You can't solve a problem with the
same mind that created it."

–Albert Einstein

There is a way out, really! There is a way out, no matter what! Sometimes we just keep trying to solve the problem with the same thinking and believe there's no way out. What you often find is that when you are in the middle of an "upset," you think you are aware of your reality, and believe that what you are feeling and what you are thinking are real and accurate.

The problem is that you are "upset." By definition, you aren't centered in your feelings, and more importantly, you often aren't centered in your thinking.

There are many reasons why you may be upset, and I won't address it all here. What you can do when you are upset is to make better decisions and think more clearly. This is the key. Sometimes you need to blow off steam, which is fine, as long as you do it without hurting anyone else or yourself.

The optimum person to help with this would be a neutral witness. This seems very hard to come by, but within each one of us, we have one. The challenge is to access our neutral witness. The ego is usually blocking us from doing this. The key is to get your ego out of the way. Once you do this, you'll be able to access this unbiased witness, the part of you that knows the answer.

First, stop what you're doing and separate yourself from what's causing your upset. Take a deep breath. Okay, now take another couple. Clear your mind for a minute. Just concentrate on your breathing. Concentrate on what's going on inside of you. Just relax and breathe. If you believe in a higher power, ask for calming clarity. Take a few minutes to center yourself.

This may be all it takes for you to be able to approach your upset and resolve the problem. Sometimes you need to release more of the energy surrounding your upset. Most often, when you can slow down for a moment, you can adjust yourself to a more centered position. When you are very off-center, you might need more than a moment. (I will cover more on how to release emotional energy in Chapter 12.) Once that release is accomplished, you may or may not be back at center. Sometimes it takes more than one process of releasing before you feel balanced, and occasionally once does it. It all depends.

If you are still out of balance, don't try to make any important decisions. Just relax and know it will get better. It's probably not as bad as it seems! There are many other methods. Choose which ones work best for you. The important thing for you to realize is everything happening to you is for your highest good; although it often doesn't seem so at the time.

There is always something to learn from each interaction in your life. The question to ask yourself is, "What can I learn from this?" Your ego will have one response, but your heart will have the answer that will benefit your highest good. Just look and see which is which. Always choose what is for your highest good. Sometimes you won't see the answer right away. Remember: Just because you can't see a way out, it doesn't mean there isn't one, two, or more! Why not believe you can find your way out? You have everything to gain!

13

"*We shall never cease from exploration*
And the end of all our exploring
Will be to arrive where we started
And know the place for the first time."

—T. S. Eliot

Useful questions:

❖ No matter how seemingly impossible, what are some of my ways out?

❖ How have I blown off steam? Are there any other, better ways to blow off steam?

❖ What is the bigger picture?

❖ What can I learn from each encounter?

Notes

Autobiography in Five Short Chapters
by Portia Nelson

1. I walk down the street
There is a deep hole in the sidewalk.
I fall in, I am lost...I am helpless.
It isn't my fault.
It takes me forever to find my way out.

2. I walk down the same street.
There is a deep hole in the sidewalk.
I pretend I don't see it, I fall in again.
I can't believe I'm in the same place.
But it isn't my fault.
It still takes me a long time to get out.

3. I walk down the same street.
There is a deep hole in the sidewalk.
I see it there; I still fall in...It's a habit.
My eyes are open.
I know where I am.
It is my fault.
I get out immediately.

4. I walk down the same street.
There is a deep hole in the sidewalk.
I walk around it.

5. I walk down another street.

"Whether you think you can or that you can't, you're usually right."

–Henry Ford

3

Miracles Happen Everyday

"Miracles are like jokes. They relieve our tension suddenly by setting us free from the chain of cause and effect."

–Gerald Branan.

Whether you believe in the law of gravity or not, it exists. The same goes for whether you believe in the law of miracles or not, miracles do happen. We are powerful creators. There is a power to create anything, and it resides in our imaginative mind. The key is you have to believe, or at least be open to a miracle happening.

Miracles come in all sizes. Many times, we don't recognize that what is happening is a miracle. It might look like a close call, or it could be a traffic jam that delays you from being involved in an accident. It might be a call from someone you were thinking about. It could be the loss of your job—where you are an unhappy employee—allowing you to change careers to something that makes your heart sing. It could be a chance meeting where you form a lifelong relationship. It could be that bike you wanted is on sale, right when you decide to buy it. The question to ask is, "What miracle do you want to happen?"

Imagine you wave a magic wand and can have ANYTHING you want. What would it be? Use your imagination. Unlimited possibilities await you. What do you want? It's okay to ask for anything. What would you ask for if you absolutely knew you'd get it? If you want to test this, think of something, anything. Get a clear picture of it in your mind. How does it look? What color is it? How does it feel? Does it have a smell or taste? Focus on this until you practically have it in your hand.

Now think of this thought several times each day. The object or situation might appear in an ad on television, or outside your window. It could show up anywhere. Someone might bring up the same object or situation to you in a conversation. Watch and see where it shows up. It will. It's a miracle.

Miracles are often created by our intention. It takes a little time. Sometimes we may have competing intentions. You can see if there is a competing intention by looking at the results. Whichever result you have, that's the intention that was strongest. If that isn't the result you wanted, you have to see what the intention was that created it.

Sometimes you say to yourself, "Well, I really want a new car, but I can't afford it." The "but I can't afford it" is winning. Look for the underlying beliefs that keep you from what you really want. Take time to focus on what you really want and write it down. Make different categories. What do you want in your professional life? What do you want in your personal life? There may be sub-categories, such as: relationships, financial, recreational, health, spiritual life, etc. Make a list for each area of your life. Now, add to your list why you "think" you can't or haven't yet been able to get these results. Look at your list of obstacles. Are they really preventing you? Is fear of something holding you back? Are you letting fear create your intentions? You choose your own beliefs. Think about it. It's true. Why not choose what you really want? Let the miracles begin!

"There are only two ways to live your life. One is as though nothing is a miracle. The other is as though everything is a miracle."

—**Albert Einstein**

Useful questions:

- ❖ What miracles have shown up in your life?

- ❖ What intentions are you telling the world?

- ❖ What do you really want that you don't have?

- ❖ What miracles would you like to have in your life?

Notes

Notes

"Where there's a will, there's a way."

—Proverb

4

Growth vs. Decay

"All growth is a leap in the dark, a
spontaneous unpremeditated act
without benefit of experience."

—Henry Miller

Socrates came up with three phases that he believed explained how humans progress through life. His idea was, we first go through a period of growth, then we plateau, then we decay. Then later, Plato came along and said we grow and decay. That's it. Basically, if you look at a tree, it's growing until someone cuts it down. Then it begins to decay. You can make a table from it—which seems like a plateau—but it's actually slowly decaying, slowly, but decaying. Humans are perpetually growing and decaying. Your cells re-grow regularly, so that literally, you are not the person you used to be. More importantly, when it comes to mentality and emotion, you are either growing or decaying.

You learn eighty percent of your "programs" (your unconscious behavior patterns,) by the time you are eight-years-old. You learn another fifteen percent by the time you're eighteen-years-old. This leaves five percent of your programs for the rest of your life.

Therefore you have an eight-year-old running your life a lot of the time, and that might not be the best for you. The good news is that you can use the five percent to change the other ninety-five percent. Some programs of your early years were key to your growth. Potty training is one example, walking is another. Often times, you create a program that works for you as a kid, but not as an adult.

You may have hid in your room to avoid dealing with someone or something, but as an adult, you must face your fears head on. Facing your fears is sometimes the last thing you want to do. Avoiding them though, doesn't make them disappear. Admitting you have fear is the first step to getting past it. Once you admit your fears, you can begin to form a plan for dealing with them. Getting support for this is one of the best ways to deal with fear successfully.

Support might be a book about how someone else faced his or her fear. It could be a friend who listens to you and encourages you to move forward. It could be a coach or therapist that you can verbalize your fears to and get advice on how to best deal with your challenges. Once you choose to deal with your fear, you begin growing again.

Sometimes you stop growing when you stop being motivated or lose hope. If you get to this place, reach for help. We all need help once in a while. Don't be afraid to ask for it. Our nature is to seek balance. Even though we may get out of balance and stop growing, it's only temporary. The good thing is you can always begin to grow again!

"True balance requires assigning realistic performance expectations to each of our roles. True balance requires us to acknowledge that our performance in some areas is more important than in others. True balance demands that we determine what accomplishments give us honest satisfaction as well as what failures cause us intolerable grief."

—Melinda M. Marshall

Useful questions:

* ❖ What areas in your life are you growing?

* ❖ What areas in your life have you been decaying?

* ❖ What areas do you want to make changes in your life?

* ❖ How will you be different when you make those changes?

Notes

Notes

"Life is like riding a bicycle. To keep your balance you must keep moving."

—Albert Einstein

5

Your Word

*"A gentleman's word is like a touch
of a whip to a racehorse."*

–Chinese Proverb

Your word is a key to how you feel about yourself. How many times have you broken your word? How many times each day do you break your word? If you think you don't break your word, answer some of these questions.

How many times in the last twenty-four hours did you say you'd do something, and you didn't do it? Perhaps it was phone calls you didn't return or promised to be on time and were late for something. Maybe you said you'd eat healthy today, or you'd work out today. Possibly you said you'd obey all traffic laws, including speeding, or that you'd spend time with someone. I could go on, but count the times you broke your word. Even if no one else knows you did, or you didn't get caught, one person knows about all of them. YOU!

Each time you break your word you lose some self-esteem. No wonder you doubt your ability to do something if you break your word daily. Your word is key to how you create your life. If you don't really believe or trust yourself, then you won't create what you really are capable of doing. Self-esteem is essential to maximizing your potential. You may convince others that you can do something, but if you have underlying self-doubt, even if it's unconscious, you will have a tough time completing what you say you want to do. Your word, and how you keep it, determines how you feel about yourself.

The good thing is that every time you keep your word, your self-esteem goes up. So the question is, "What is your word worth?" Every time you break your word, how do you justify your actions? Think about it for a minute. No matter how good you are at defending your actions, a part of you knows you broke your word. No justification will change that. You can't fool yourself. It's your choice to keep your word or not.

Some people don't break their word because they don't commit to anything. This is one of those kid's programs that as an adult, doesn't work. This is usually done unconsciously. If you find yourself not committing to others, chances are you aren't committing to yourself either. Not committing is self-defeating. If you don't commit to anything, what can you ever achieve?

Commitment is essential to achievement. You might say that you don't break your word, but not committing to anything is simply not facing your fear. You don't have to be perfect. Non-commitment is trying to be just that, perfect. Being human by definition is not perfect. Making commitments and not always keeping them is human. Striving to be the best you can is all that's required. It's never too late to change. Self-respect and self-esteem are built on your word. Now you choose what you want to give your word to. How high do you want your self-esteem to be? You choose!

"Words have the power to both destroy and heal. When words are both true and kind, they can change our world."

—Buddha

Useful questions:

❖ How have you broken your word?

❖ How have you justified breaking your word?

❖ How can you keep your word more often?

❖ What do you want your word to be worth?

Notes

Notes

"Be true to your work, your word, and your friend."

—Henry David Thoreau

6

Fear vs. Desire

"Desire is creation, the magical element in that process. If there were an instrument by which to measure desire, one could foretell achievement."

–Godfrey St. Peter

Humans are motivated by two factors, fear and desire. These are opposite of each other, but sometimes work together. When you do something, you are motivated by one or the other, and once in a while, by both. You go to work to get paid. That is, you desire money or what it buys. You might also go to work because you're afraid of getting fired and losing what you desire.

Sometimes you avoid something out of fear, like swimming away from a shark. Fear isn't always this obvious. Sometimes you don't consciously know you have fear. Sometimes it's just a feeling of discomfort about a situation or person. Fear isn't a bad thing. In fact, it's often a great protector of us. But sometimes fear holds you back from something you want. This is one way where you may have conflicting intentions. You may want a relationship but be afraid of getting hurt.

Look at your results if you want to know which are stronger. Results are not always what we want to look at, but they are always fair. This is where desire can overcome fear. If your desire is more powerful than your fear, you'll create what you want.

Often times there are multiple intentions involved, and sorting through them may take a while, especially if you don't even consciously know what they are. It's not always important to know what the specific fears are, but sometimes it helps to recognize it when it comes up, so you can consciously choose what you want or how to respond from a place of knowing. The simple way to get around this is to build up the clear intention of exactly what you do want.

The key is being very specific and detailed as to stating what you want. Do you really know what you want, or are you just clear about what you don't want? There's a big difference between the two. In either case, it's most important to get clear about what you really want.

There are times when you feel you need a change of something outside of you. Like a new job, a new relationship, a new place to live. Maybe you just want a break, a vacation, or just to get away. The problem with this is that wherever you go, you're still there. That is, YOU are still there. The change you're looking for has to come from inside out.

Let's try something. Get a piece of paper and pen. Begin by imagining you have twenty million dollars, and whatever skills you need can be taught. Also, know you won't fail at whatever you choose to do. Now, what do you want? Ask yourself, "What do I want?" Be as detailed as possible. Just write down whatever comes up, no matter how weird it may sound. Keep asking and writing anything that comes forward for you. Do this until you fill up at least a page of desires.

Once you have your list, go through each one, and write down how you'll feel when you fulfill that desire. Write it as if you already have it. If you want a new car, what kind? What color? What options? For example, use something like this. "I am driving my new blue, fully- loaded BMW 5 Series up the Pacific Coast Highway, with the 12-CD

45

changer playing my favorite songs." If you want to travel, where do you want to go? With whom do you want to go?" For how long? If you want a new relationship, how would that look? How would it make you feel? Paint a picture with words. Use action-oriented adjectives and descriptive adverbs, like, "I am happily jet skiing with the woman of my dreams." Or, "I am ecstatically exchanging love daily through heartfelt communication." Do this for every aspect of your life. What you will get by doing this is empowerment. Your subconscious mind doesn't know the difference between pretending and reality. As far as it's concerned, both are "real." Your thoughts create your reality. There is power in your word and more power in your written word. Write at least a paragraph for each desire. Ask yourself, "What do you really want from each choice?" Are you surprised by any of your desires? Are there any underlying wants that might not be directly connected to your desire? You may desire a new job, but really want to be able to express yourself more creatively. Can that be done in your present job? Maybe, maybe not. The only way to find out is to explore the possibilities. Maybe you desire a new relationship, but really want to be loved and supported. Can that be done in your present relationship? Again, maybe yes, maybe no.

Are you beginning to sort out your desires? You have the choice to dream for anything. Why not paint a winning picture? After all, it's your dream! Once you are clear about your desires, write them down and put them where you can see them daily. Read them out loud often. Watch it work!

"Our deepest fear is not that we are inadequate. "Our deepest fear is that we are powerful beyond measure. It is our light not our darkness that most frightens us. We ask ourselves, who am I to be brilliant, gorgeous, talented, and fabulous? Actually, who are you not to be? You are a child of God. Your playing small does not serve the world. There is nothing enlightened about shrinking so that other people around you won't feel insecure. We were born to make manifest the glory of God that is within us. It is not just in some of us; it is in everyone. As we let our own light shine, we unconsciously give other people permission to do the same. As we are liberated from our own fear, our presence automatically liberates others."

—Marianne Williamson

Useful questions:

❖ What have I been truly afraid of?

❖ Are any of these fears valid?

❖ What do I really desire in my life?

❖ How will I be when I have what I really want?

Notes

Notes

"*Desire is half of life, indifference is half of death.*"

—Kahlil Gibran

7

Anger

Holding on to anger is like grasping a hot coal with the intent of throwing it at someone else; you are the one who gets burned.

– Buddha

Anger is not good or bad. It just is. How you deal with anger is the key to the outcome. Anger management is not just not showing your anger. Many people who need anger management do need to adjust their display of anger. Part of their problem is they have a lot of anger stored up and it may show up in different ways, often misunderstood.

Imagine that you are a battery. You are. In this case, your charge is either positive or negative charge. Okay, you might have neutral charge, but that is rare and usually takes a lot of emotional healing work. So there you are with your charge. What it is depends on your past experiences. Part of your past experiences include those around you and their charges. Because as children, we are sponges. We absorb everything around us to learn about life. That includes the energies of those around us. So if someone had a negative charge, whether they expressed it or not, you might have absorbed it. Let me explain it this way.

Imagine you and someone close to you are batteries. When you are in a relationship of any kind your batteries are connected invisibly like jumper cables between two cars. Energy can be exchanged subconsciously. That is why you can be around someone who is not demonstrating anger or another emotion, and you sense something. It might be comfort or discomfort. You don't know why, but you feel one or the other and will engage or distance yourself from the source. This can even be felt over the phone, and when you hang up it breaks the connection. This all may sound a little strange but pay attention to your encounters and see if you consciously can pick up on the energy exchange.

For those who are sensitive to energy exchange you may need to recharge your own energy by being alone. If you don't pay attention to people's energy, you may find yourself feeling and expressing their energy as if it is your own. It will feel just as if it is yours, but may have no connection to you, just a feeling. If you watch a commercial or a movie and are feeling like one of the characters or start crying during a sad or emotional scene, you are feeling the emotion of that character. Advertisers count on that. They want to manipulate you to buy their product or see their movie, etc.

Imagine that you have a negative "charge" of a minus 6 from the past. Then something occurs in the present similar to that and it is a minus 4. The two combine and you feel a minus 10 of upset, and you respond to a minus 10. The person on the receiving end knows they don't deserve a minus 10 response and thus begins the war of misunderstanding. Both parties feel "right" in their feelings. And technically they are both right in what they feel. They misunderstanding is the hidden minus 6 added to the equation. Until that is uncovered and removed it is hard to heal the rift caused. In fact this may contribute to build up of another minus 6 with the other party. And so it goes until an explosion or demolition of the hidden charges. If it goes on long enough the minuses might be more like minus 250 or more. Long term resentment builds up and forgiveness is harder to find.

This is science. It happens all the time. Some people are more sensitive to it and need to pay more attention to their surroundings. Many misunderstandings occur when this happens. For example, when someone sensitive and good at expressing their emotions encounters someone who denies or pushes down their emotions a scene plays out. The sensitive one expresses the emotions of the suppressed person, sometime at the suppressed person and it looks like the sensitive one is the upset one. In reality it is the suppressed person who is upset and unwilling or unable to express their emotions in a positive way. Thus the sensitive person looks like they need anger management when it is the other person who does.

Sometimes the suppressed person knows all about their anger but is too afraid of expressing it for fear of "losing it completely." They have learned to cope with shutting off the emotions to survive. They don't even realize it has become normal to hold it in. They have noticed that it builds up making it more likely to become a major explosion whenever it is set off. So down it goes inside. If it isn't dealt with consciously it will find a way to come out. It often turns into dis-ease. It may show up as illness.

In other cases it is passed on to those around you, including children and animals. Children and animals don't have the ability to block it, so they express it or run away. If you have ever noticed this kind of behavior in kids or pets it is a sign to do some of your own emotional work.

There are various ways to express your anger in a healthy way. Unfortunately, many times when you feel angry, you are not feeling like letting it go in a healthy manor. But stuffing it down is not good either. Once you begin letting it go in a healthy way, the stored anger is no longer the contributing factor that it was.

See Chapter 12 on Forgiveness for ways to let go of anger in a healthy way.

Useful questions:

- ❖ What has triggered my anger?

- ❖ How do I deal with my anger?

- ❖ Who do I need to forgive in my life?

- ❖ How can I let go of my upsets in a healthy way?

Notes

Don't hold to anger, hurt, or pain. They steal your energy and keep you from love.

- Leo Buscaglia

8

Criticism vs. Encouragement

"Any fool can criticize, condemn, and complain but it takes character and self-control to be understanding and forgiving."

– Dale Carnegie

B est results come when people feel good about themselves. What do you think works best, criticism or encouragement? Well, if you don't know, it's encouragement. Criticism does little to improve someone's performance. In fact, usually it defeats the person's desire to succeed, either consciously or unconsciously. There are some people who respond to criticism by upping their performance, but they're the minority. For most, being criticized reduces confidence and therefore lessons their performance.

I am one of the majority here. I become better when encouraged. Positive statements lift me up. When I believe in myself, I can overcome obstacles, even sizeable ones. Why would anyone choose to criticize rather than encourage? Basically, it usually comes from upbringing. They were criticized as children and learned to succeed to avoid it. Therefore they think it is a useful tool to use. Unfortunately, when it is used on people who resent criticism it backfires! The rebels will do the exact opposite of what the criticizer wants. Neither really gets the success they both desire. The ones who failed to succeed because of the criticism will most likely also fail this time too.

This is the kind of topic that needs to be discussed in advance of whatever performance is required. However, sometimes it is only under the stress of the performance that the issue arises. It is too late then. The damage is done. The criticizer will blame the failure on the other performer. Often the performer will believe that he/she was at fault. But in reality, it is the criticizer who deserves the blame. They instigated the downturn in performance with their criticism and blame. Unless this is seen and brought up by a neutral observer, chances are no improvement will occur.

Because people shun blame, they will shift it onto others. Depending on the situation, the person blamed might be able to bring up the topic and initiate new behavior from the criticizer. But if the criticizer refuses to accept blame, the problem will continue. There has to be give and take for understanding and improvement to take place.

My advice is to be open to discussing any difference of opinion and if needed, have a neutral observer moderate the discussion. Many times our upbringing works for us personally, but not professionally or with others. Learn what works for the others that you connect with. It may be completely different that you think. Criticism is important in certain circumstances. Learn what works and what doesn't. It will allow the best of each person to shine.

"*I have yet to find the man, however exalted his station, who did not do better work and put forth greater effort under a spirit of approval than under a spirit of criticism.*"

– Charles Schwab

9

How to Change Your Mind

"Like all weak men, he laid an exaggerated stress on not changing one's mind."

—W. Somerset Maugham

P eople say a mind is a terrible thing to waste.

They're right! More specifically, not using your mind is a terrible waste. We all use some of our mind's abilities, and we all use more of our mind's subconscious than we're aware. For example, have you ever driven somewhere and after doing so wonder how you got there because, you weren't paying attention? In cases like this, your subconscious mind drove you. Luckily, we have a very powerful and talented subconscious mind. You don't have to remember how to brush your teeth each time you do so. You don't have to remember how to talk; okay maybe some of us do. We don't have to remember how to eat, or walk, or any of a number of repetitive things we have learned. Our subconscious mind knows, remembers, and does so many things for us. An expression to describe this is, "It's like riding a bike," which means that once you've learned to ride, that knowledge will still be there.

Most of us think we have only learned to use the basic subconscious mind. In reality, we use the subconscious mind daily for much more than we know. If you meet someone and you "feel" good about them, it's your subconscious mind at work. If you're hoping for something and by "coincidence" that thing shows up, it's your subconscious mind at work.

You've been creating your life as you go.

Sometimes there's more than your mind at work in this creative process. Just know that we are all capable of creating lots of things in our lives. It's important to know what you are creating, so if you want something else, you need to make sure you have one clear intention and release any competing ones.

Unless it's something new you want. If you don't have it, you probably have a competing intention, or belief, that has kept you from attaining what you want.

Sometimes you actually get something better than you wanted. As long as you're okay with "better," it works for you. If, for some reason, you have a limiting belief about something, even if you get it, you'll probably lose it, unless you change your belief. Sometimes you might have a "goodness" ceiling. Once you hit that level of "goodness," of things going your way, or good fortune, you subconsciously sabotage yourself to keep you "safe" in your comfort zone. Ask yourself how good can you stand to feel? Notice how many lottery winners lose all of it within five years.

Sometimes you fear failure, sometimes success, and many times, it's on a subconscious level. What you believe on a conscious level may not agree with your subconscious level. The important thing is, do you like what you're getting? As Dr. Phil McGraw says, "How's that working for you?" Assuming you want something different than you have, do you consciously feel you deserve it? If you do, and you don't have it, are you really clear about what it is that you want? If you say, for example, "I want more money." Is twenty-five cents enough? That's more money, after all.

Your intention or goal needs to be S.M.A.R.T.(Specific, Measurable, Appropriate, Realistic, and have a finite measurement of Time.) Take Specific for example. How much more money do you want? When you say, "I want to have one hundred thousand dollars per year income before taxes by the end of this year," that's specific. It's also Measurable. Appropriate has to do with several factors. Does it meet your needs and wants? Does it interfere with someone else's? Think of the interference like this, "I want to be in a relationship with Mary," versus, "I want to be in a romantic relationship with a loving woman like Mary." You may or may not be in a relationship with Mary, but as far as intentions are concerned, Mary's life is her own. Remember, you might get that or something better, so don't limit yourself!

Realistic is a little grayer area. Realistic is about believability, your believability with your goal. A good rule of thumb is to make your intention fifty percent believable or fifty percent unbelievable, whichever works for you. So, if making fifty thousand dollars is believable by the end of the year, then one hundred thousand dollars is fifty percent believable. One million dollars is not realistic, at least not in one year. In five years, however, it could be realistic. It could still happen, but stretching your reality and your comfort zone to that level might be more challenging. There is a reasonable finite measurement of Time to this goal as well, so we have all the elements. Try it yourself with various parts of your life. See if you change your mind and start getting what you want.

Make sure you use these goals as guideposts to keep you on track. If you find you're off, just adjust your effort or your goals to fit.

"The secret of getting ahead is getting started. The secret of getting started is breaking your complex overwhelming tasks into small manageable tasks, and then starting on the first one."

—Mark Twain

Useful questions:

* ❖ What are my intentions?

* ❖ Do I have any competing intentions?

* ❖ If so, what are they?

* ❖ What do I believe about me?

Notes

Notes

"To think is to create"

—Napoleon Hill.

10

Take Back Your Power

*"Everything can be taken from a man
but...the last of the human
freedoms—to choose one's attitude in
any given set of circumstances, to
choose one's own way."*

–Viktor E. Frankl

S ometimes you don't realize you have the power to create the life you want, even if you are willing to use it. You may feel powerless when life sometimes presents you with events which you have no control in bringing about. As we discussed earlier about having intentions, you create your life. How you create your life is up to you. Sometimes you really want something and you don't create it. Like the words from a Garth Brooks song, "Unanswered Prayers," sometimes you discover later, there was something better you didn't even consciously know about. Only afterward can you look back and see that it was better. What you have to realize is, there is a bigger picture, and you're sometimes too close to see the whole picture. Like a puzzle, as you add pieces, you tend to get a better idea of what you're creating. This is one of the pieces. How you put them together is up to you.

One thing that can keep you from connecting to your power is addictions. Addictions have their own agenda, and it's in direct opposition to your power. Addictions run from the classic substance addiction, to the behavioral. Some people are addicted to TV or the Internet. Behavioral addictions aren't often recognized or acknowledged. Regardless of what you use to avoid reality, it does have a cost. Making decisions when under the influence of your addiction is usually not for your highest good. When you are under the influence, your guilt center is removed temporarily, and replaced with the "I want" mechanism. The "I want" could be most anything depending on the addiction. The bottom line will be, "I want to satisfy my needs," which include feeding the addiction, and any other "self-medicating" behavior that makes you "feel safe." This often makes you "feel nothing," that is numbing your emotions.

This is why overweight people eat, even when they're full. They are "looking for love in all the wrong places." They are literally trying to satisfy their need for love and safety. Addiction is not dealing with reality. Its answer may only satisfy the individual for the moment, and sometimes not even then. It's a response of feeling "out of control." That is, you may feel, "I don't have the ability to control getting what I want." That is the basic error, believing you don't have the ability to get what you want. Believing that you can change is the key to creating this. You do have the power to change. You have the responsibility. Therefore, you have the ability to choose how you respond! That's the good news! You can create something different than what you have now. But you need to choose differently than you have in the past.

Sometimes we cling to our status quo for fear of the unknown. This is often what keeps us stuck. We'd rather keep what we know, even though we don't like it, than what we don't know. That is when fate steps in.

When we need to move forward in life, but refuse, a crisis comes along. A crisis is a gift, although it often may seem just the opposite at first. A crisis is an opportunity for transforming your life. A crisis takes you out of your comfort zone. You get caught up in blaming. Lots of "shoulds" come up, like, "It should be different. It should be better. I shouldn't have to deal with this."

The real challenge is fear. When you can face your fear, you can create the life you really want. Moving through your fear is the key to getting what you want. Fear is a valuable and useful part of life, but sometimes, you may use it as a reason to hold you back in your life. How you choose to relate to fear will determine how you'll create your reality. Don't let fear stop you from getting what you really want. Instead, focus on what you want. Why not choose to put your energy on the goal you want? You'll find that the more you focus on the goal, the less fear will have on you.

Taking back your power means to claim your life for what you want it to be. Start taking back your power by taking responsibility for your life. Remember, to claim responsibility, claims your power. You have the ability to change your life.

You have to make the choice to change. Once you do, your life will shift. You don't have to know how to make it all happen. You just have to be clear of what you really want. This comes from your heart, not your head. Only you can keep yourself from getting what you really want.

Once you are in alignment with your heart, your life will move forward and everything you need will show up.

If you're still having trouble getting in touch with what it is you really want, try to take time to sit and be quiet with the intention of having what you really want come to you. Do this daily if you can. Once you have a clear picture of what you really want, close your eyes. Imagine you have achieved your goals. Feel what it feels like. How are you feeling? How are you being different? Remember how it feels, and how you are being. Begin each day with a few minutes of "remembering" this feeling. Sit quietly and just focus your attention on this feeling as if it were true now. Watch how you're being shifted to match this. It will. Your mind will make it so.

"It often takes a crisis to break through our usual models of the world. A crisis is a gift, an opportunity, and perhaps a manifestation that life loves us, by beckoning us to go beyond the dance we presently perform."

–Leslie Lebeau

Useful questions:

* ❖ How have I given my power away?

* ❖ How will I handle fear when it comes up?

* ❖ What kind of help do I need to achieve my goals?

* ❖ How will I be when I have achieved my goals?

Notes

Notes

"We have met the enemy, and he is us!"
—from the comic strip Pogo

by Walt Kelly

11

Aligning With Your Subconscious Mind

"The Subconscious mind cannot tell the difference between what's real and what's imagined."

– Bob Proctor

When you have consciously desired something and after 6 months you have not made any progress toward achieving it, your subconscious mind desires something else, AND it's winning! The reason it wins is, it knows your conscious mind, but if you don't pay attention, it will run its program to achieve what it thinks is the right result. It thinks it is doing what you want because on the subconscious level you do want it. There may be different reasons for that belief, but until you change its programming, you will find it very difficult to achieve your conscious desires.

There are several ways to find out what your subconscious mind desires. I will explain some here. The easiest way is to look at your results. That is what it desires. Why is another question. If you want those answers it will you will have to ask. Counselling with a coach or therapist is one way to uncover them. But some people don't want to do that for one reason or another. So, I will offer other ways to discover the underlying reasons here.

Journalling at least 4 days a week for several weeks can offer some possible answers. Usually there will develop a pattern of reasons. When you want to do this just before bed. First do a "brain dump". This is where you write down any thoughts no matter how mundane they may be. Write anything you think you need to remember for the next day. This clears out your mind because you no longer need to hold those thoughts since you wrote them down.

Then begin with an intention. Tell your subconscious mind that you want the answers to *such and such* (whatever you want answers to) to come to you in a clear fashion, with grace and ease. The with grace and ease is important because some answers can come with a lot of impact if you don't ask for the softer way. Sometimes the answers will come to you in a dream. Have a pen and paper near your bed so you can write down any information that might come to you in the middle of the night. Then the next morning begin by sitting quietly for at least five minutes. Then begin writing. Write down whatever thoughts come to you. Initially they might not make sense, but soon a pattern comes forward. It may take some time and you might need help discerning their meaning, but answers will come.

Another way to connect with your subconscious mind is called non-dominant handwriting. To do this take a pen and paper and using your dominant hand, write the question that you want answers to on the paper. Then switch the pen to your non-dominant hand and let it answer. Do not judge the penmanship. It has had much less practice after all. The answers will come. You might have to ask more than once until you trigger the response that you are looking for. When it comes out you will know it's true. This may take some practice, but it can become a valuable way to discover the unconscious motivations that you have.

Once you have the answers, "Now what?" Well, I'm glad you asked. Your subconscious mind tracks everything that you say and do. It knows if you keep your word. Remember Chapter 5? Yup your word is how to align with your subconscious mind. I have developed a simple process to get your subconscious mind to work with you. Notice I said simple, not easy. In reality it can be easy, but that is up to you. I call it ADGRs.

ADGRs are Absolute Daily Goals with Rewards. To create an ADGR break down a bigger goal that you have. Let's use releasing weight as an example. My bigger goal is to exercise 30 minutes a day for six days a week. But an ADGR is something that you can accomplish in one minute or less. So in this case I choose to do one sit-up. Yes, that's it, one sit-up. So if 11:59 at night rolls around and I had forgotten to do my ADGR, I can get down on the floor and do my one sit-up, et voila! I have accomplished my goal for the day. I chose something that I absolutely knew I could do, no matter what. Once you do one sit-up you will probably do a set of 10. And then you're off to completing a workout, but you only committed to one sit-up.

Now to reward myself. I know why should I reward myself for only doing one sit-up? Well I will tell you since you asked. 80% of your subconscious programming happens by the time you are 8 years old. Another 15% by the time you are 18 years old. So you have 5% left for the rest of your life. Luckily, you can reprogram the other 95% with your 5% if you know how. This is how. Basically an 8 year old is running you most of the time. This works in many ways, and yet can have challenges depending on your experiences and your decisions made at that time. Of course your experiences and decisions the rest of your life also come to play in your life, so you need to consider all of it. For now, just accept that an 8 year old wants to be rewarded for doing something, no matter how small. So reward you will.

Interestingly enough this is the hardest part of the ADGR process for most people. So I encourage you to write out 12 rewards on a piece of paper and post it somewhere. Then when you cannot think of a reward, you can just point to one and do that. Now you cannot have "Eat an entire carton of ice-cream" as a reward, especially if you want to release weight. You might have things on the list like a ten-minute call with a person I care about. Or perhaps listening to my favorite CD. Even a walk in nature could be a great reward. Write your list and use it daily. Once you begin to use this process you will find things you want to accomplish become easier. Your subconscious mind does not know size of goals. It just knows if you kept your word or not. Once you build up a record of keeping your word, your subconscious mind will join in and align with your conscious mind's desires.

Useful questions:

* ❖ What results do I want to be different?

* ❖ How will I handle fear when it comes up?

* ❖ What has my subconscious mind wanted instead of my conscious mind's desires?

* ❖ What are some rewards that I can use for my ADGRs?

Notes

Notes

"Your subconscious mind makes all your words and actions fit a pattern consistent with your self-concept and your innermost beliefs about yourself."

– Brian Tracy

12

Forgiveness

*"Forgiving is the pathway to
happiness and the quickest way to
undo suffering and pain."*

–Gerald Jampolsky, M.D

F orgiveness is so important. The biggest obstacle we
have to getting the life we want is ourselves. Holding
onto the past hurts and keeps us victims. Forgiveness is
what allows us to move forward, past our own mental
blocks. Forgiveness means to "give as before." This isn't
about continuing a relationship with someone that may
have hurt you. Often it's just the opposite. As long as you
hold onto pain from someone that hurt you, you are
connected to that person.

By releasing the resentment and the anger through the act of forgiveness, you are disconnecting from the pain that person may have caused. This doesn't mean you are condoning the behavior of someone who hurt you; it's about you letting go of the need to blame and therefore, your need to suffer. It's not about forgiving others so much as it's about forgiving ourselves.

You may need to forgive others, but it doesn't have to do with them. It's all about you. It's about how you feel. If you harbor anger from some past hurt, it hurts you to keep hanging onto it, and it will often show up in some physical illness in you. It can become disease.

Forgiveness is about releasing the pain that you've kept inside of you. The way to release is by expressing all of the feelings you have attached to it.

One technique to do this is what I call the Soul Letter process. This is where you write your feelings down to express them. I've given you lead-in lines for you to complete. Like "I'm so angry that..." Give it a try.

Don't worry if you don't know what you're feeling. This can help you sort out what's really inside you. Often you'll feel releases as you go through the writing process. You might want to have some tissues or a pillow nearby. Use what works for you. Whatever comes up is okay. There are no wrong answers here. If you feel overwhelmed to the point of an inability to function, or feel you'd prefer to have someone personally guide you, seek professional help from a licensed therapist. If you do see a therapist, bring these Soul Letters with you. It may serve to offer insight and speed your healing process.

I have put the sections in the normal order that you will feel the emotions. However, sometimes women in particular, may find the first emotion they feel is sadness rather than anger. If you feel that more, begin with the Sadness and Wounds section, then do the Blame and Upset section. After that, continue as the remaining rest of the outline suggests.

Remember it's important to express all of your emotions, and not judge them (or yourself) as you go through this process. Don't edit, or worry about spelling or punctuation. Swear if you want and remember to express yourself fully. These are not to be shared*, they are just for you! Make sure you go all the way through this process, so you complete the emotional release.

*These letters are not for sharing. These are intended to help you to heal and connect to your higher Self through Forgiveness.

*You may choose to share this letter, ONLY if the other person knows this process and agrees to share it, otherwise use it just for you or you can share these with your coach or therapist.

Just keep repeating the lines and filling in the blanks until you uncover the truth of your feelings.

Soul Letter

Seven Steps to Truth

1. Blame and Upset

Express your feelings without judgment

I am so angry that...I'm so upset that...

2. Sadness and Wounds

I'm sad that...It hurt me when...

3. Doubt and Fear

(This is the KEY level; this is what's really bothering you)

I don't know if...I'm afraid that...

4. Responsibility and Guilt

(Here's where you dump your guilt for anything you've said, done or not done)

I'm sorry that I...I didn't mean...

5. Judgment and Forgiveness

I forgive myself for believing myself as...

I forgive myself for believing _____ as...

6. Hopes and Wishes

(If you could wave a magic wand, what would you like to have happen?)

I wish that...I hope that...

Add "This or something better for the highest good of all concerned."

7. Truth and Love

(Here's where you express your truth, love, appreciation, and respect.)

I love you for...I appreciate that...

The truth is...I respect you for...

I've used Soul Letters to help dump lots of emotional baggage. I have written these more to myself than to anyone else. The reason is that no one is as mad at you as you. Using the Soul Letters help you get rid of negative voices in your head; the ones that always say, "You can't", the ones that criticize you. It really works!

Some other suggested recipients might be: mom, dad, sister, brother, boss, ex-boyfriend, ex-girlfriend, ex-spouse, etc.

Sometimes you may have to write more than one letter to the same person. Don't try to solve thirty years of upset in one letter. Keep about two pages maximum per section and try to keep the sections relatively balanced. Remember, these are just for you. This gives you the freedom to express what you are really feeling.

Don't share them with the recipient. That often makes things worse. You may even want to tear them up or burn them to feel additional release, or you can just hit your delete key!

One secret to doing this exercise—when someone may see what you're writing—is to use only the first letter of each word. It's gibberish to the average person, and you can write faster. It is sometimes harder to reread (if that's necessary for you), but you can write them right in front of the person it's directed to without them knowing what you're doing! Try it! It really works!

"Forgive us our trespasses, as we forgive those who trespass against us."

—The Lord's Prayer

Useful questions:

- ❖ What areas have I been stuck in?

- ❖ Who do I need to forgive?

- ❖ What do I need to forgive myself for?

Notes

"Forgiveness is the answer to the child's dream of a miracle, by which what is broken is made whole again, what is soiled is made clean again."

—Dag Hammarskjold

13

Commitment

*"Commitment is healthiest when it's not
without doubt, but in spite of doubt."*

—Rollo May PhD

C ommitment to yourself is the key to making change
last. Commitment begins with deciding a goal that
is S.M.A.R.T. Once you have chosen your goals, write
them down, and verify that they meet all the S.M.A.R.T.
criteria. Now that you know where you want to end up,
go back from there, and determine what objectives you'll
have to meet along the way to create the results you want.

Break them down in reasonably timed pieces. Break them
into monthly, weekly, and daily tasks, keeping the
S.M.A.R.T. criteria in mind. When you have the objectives
broken down in small pieces, you need to commit yourself

to doing them and to the specific action steps. Make sure you build in guideposts of objectives needed to reach your goal to determine if you are on track.

Commitment begins the instant you decide, really decide, something. What does it take to do that? How much does it mean to you? What if you look ten years down the road and nothing in your life has changed? How would you feel? How long will it take you to decide to do something different in your life? How long are you willing to wait? What if nothing has changed in five years?

How will you feel then? Time moves quicker than you think. How long will you wait? If nothing changed in a year, what then? Are you willing to take that chance? How long has it been since you knew you needed a change? How much more time are you willing to wait? Another month? Nothing changing? Another week? Another day? Another hour?

Or can you change NOW? Commit NOW? Choose NOW? Decide you want something better in your life NOW! Don't wait. Make the decision to shift your thinking NOW! Commit NOW! To quote the Nike shoe company slogan: "Just Do It." NOW! Commitment is powerful. It's a declaration to the world that you intend to do something. Miracles happen with commitment.

Once you've truly committed to yourself and to your goals, you will achieve them, as long as you believe you can. If you need help believing, just remember all the people who went before you. They created so much more than anyone would have ever believed. Landing a man on the moon began with a belief that we could. It began long before we knew how. It began with commitment.

On September 12, 1962, President John F. Kennedy stated, "We choose to go to the moon. We choose to go to the moon in this decade and do the other things, not because they are easy, but because they are hard, because that goal will serve to organize and measure the best of our energies and skills, because that challenge is one that we are willing to accept, one we are unwilling to postpone, and one which we intend to win, and the others, too." The President convinced others to believe with him, that it could be done. On July 20, 1969, when Astronaut Neil Armstrong took his, "One small step for man and one giant leap for mankind," that remark defined intention, belief, and commitment.

Belief in yourself and belief in your goals is free. Why not choose to believe? Why not win in your own dream? Are you ready to go for it? Yes? Great! Now that you've committed to your goals, build support around you to help you to succeed. Find people you can depend on for positive support. Start with family or friends. Remember you want support, not ridicule. Choose people you can depend on to believe with you. If you want more support, a helpful source can be found at http://www.johnseeleyma.com. Or you can start your own Get Unstuck Now group!

"Life takes on meaning when you become motivated, set goals and charge after them in an unstoppable manner."

—Les Brown

Useful questions:

- ❖ What are my S.M.A.R.T. goals for each area of my life?

- ❖ How can I get past what has stopped me from attaining goals in the past?

- ❖ What steps am I committing to taking?

- ❖ Who is in my support team?

Notes

"Do what you can with what you have where you are."

—Theodore Roosevelt

14

Gratitude

"You don't know what you got till it's gone. They paved paradise and put up a parking lot."

--Joni Mitchell

G ratitude is something that changes how you feel about everything. Start by being grateful for what you already have. Watch how you begin to feel differently about what you have. Gratitude helps you to come from a place of having, vs. a place of lack. Too often we take what we have for granted. Recognition of the quality, value, significance, or magnitude of people and things is what true appreciation is.

Once you learn to really appreciate everything you have, far beyond material possessions, real gratitude begins.

Start by appreciating each breath you take, the warmth of the sun, the smile of a friend or the laugh of a child. Being consciously grateful gives you a feeling of wealth and deservability and contributes to your life.

Understanding how gratitude works isn't necessary; just know it does. It's like a time I remember when I was a kid. My dad gave me an allowance for doing chores. I spent it all in one day. I asked my dad for more. He said I'd have to learn to appreciate what I had first, before he'd give me anymore. That's how life works for adults, too. You have to appreciate what you have, no matter what it is, before it gives you more.

I remember when I was first introduced to this concept. I started writing a gratitude journal every night before I went to bed. I committed to writing a minimum of three things I was grateful for. This was at a time in my life when I didn't really have much to be grateful for, and I sometimes struggled to find three things. Often my entries would be, "I'm grateful that I'm alive. I'm grateful I had something to eat today. I'm grateful it didn't rain today." Things started getting better.

Now I have much more to be grateful for, but it all began with the basics. I could go on and write many pages on what I am now grateful for, but what is more important is for you to think about what you're grateful for.

Think about what you have now. Write a list of fifty things you are grateful for. For some people that might be easy, for others hard. Which is it for you? It's easy to ask for more, but first realize what you have—no matter how much that is—is a gift. You helped to create it, and you can help to create more.

I've had the chance to see others with more money and less happiness, and less money and more happiness. What do you value most? If you have a roof over your head, food to eat, a safe place to sleep, and the ability to say what you want, you are better off than ninety-five percent of the world. Instead of taking what you have for granted, learn to appreciate everything you do have. It's easy to get caught up in the, "look what someone else has compared to me," syndrome.

Remember we only "rent" everything on this planet. Except for love, you can't take it with you. Do you appreciate the people in your life? Often you don't realize what you have until it's taken away. That's a hard way to learn how to be grateful. Unfortunately, that's how some of us must learn. Worse yet, sometimes that's when you don't feel grateful at all. How you face change is up to you. It's a choice that can change your life in a positive way if you want it to. It's up to you. Just do it.

"No one is as capable of gratitude as one who has emerged from the kingdom of night."

–Elie Wiesel

Useful questions:

- ❖ What things do I have to be grateful for daily, and why?

- ❖ Who am I grateful to have in my life, and why?

- ❖ What things about me I am grateful for?

Notes

"Gratitude is not only the greatest of virtues, but the parent of all others."

—Cicero

15

The Next Step

"They always say time changes things, but you actually have to change them yourself."

–Andy Warhol

Moving forward in your life can be scary, because doing so is taking you out of your comfort zone. If after you begin to make some positive changes and feel uncomfortable or feel fear coming up, that's great! This means you are stepping out of your comfort zone, and changing your patterns, which allows you to change what you have in your life. Everything you want but don't have is outside of your present comfort zone.

Trusting yourself and the process, while believing you can attain what you desire, is all you need. Growth doesn't always feel pleasant, but the outcome will lead to positive results. Little steps at first are all that are required.

Here are some suggestions to get you started:

- Begin with something like writing in your "gratitude journal" each night. Write three things you are grateful for.
- Begin taking five minutes in the morning to sit and be quiet. Listen to your inner wisdom. If you begin getting a consistent message, follow through on it. See what happens.
- Take five minutes to appreciate someone in your life.
- Take a walk in nature. Notice everything that surrounds you.
- Begin journaling. Write down your feelings and thoughts at least four times a week. Watch for patterns that emerge in your journaling. The simple act of "paying attention" often helps you to notice what's been in front of you for years. You may be surprised to find how simple it can be to find what you need to change and create.
- Write down what you want to create in your life. Write your S.M.A.R.T. goals and create a plan to achieve these goals. Break your plan into daily,

weekly, and monthly action steps. Get Unstuck Now!

- Build in guideposts to let you know if you're on track. Make adjustments as needed. Be open to fine tuning your goals along the way.
- Let go of the goals that no longer fit and create new ones as your perception about life shifts.
- Make sure you keep balance in your life. Feed your emotional, spiritual, mental, and physical sides to reach your weekly goals.
- Be true to yourself. Learn to love and accept yourself. Learn to love and accept others. Learn to love life.
- Build a support team of positive loving people.
- Build in rewards along the way.

Congratulations on making it through this book! You have already taken positive steps toward changing your life. Remember...never underestimate the power of your thoughts to create new possibilities! As you follow the suggestions in this book, you will find much of the clarity you have been seeking. You have all the tools you need inside YOU! You also have the ability to make changes in your life to begin creating the life you really want. Share this with others. You may find helping others will help you as well.

You have gone from a feeling of being stuck, to knowing what you want to change in your life. You have an understanding of what you can do to move forward and make positive changes in your life. You have found ways to take your power back by developing new habits of keeping your word. You now have tools for creating the life you truly desire through focus, forgiveness, and gratitude.

Finally, you have committed to making new choices, and to demonstrate gratitude for what you have. Remember, YOU are courageous. Reach for your dreams. Believe it is possible to create the life you are dreaming of and MORE!

This book is a tool. Use it as a reference guide, over and over, to free you up whenever you or someone you know is "stuck" in life. Keep it with you, and reference it anytime you're feeling the need to change. I hope it will bring you to the place you want to be in your life. Take the action steps that make sense to you.

Be gentle with yourself as you go through this process. Make your life what you really want it to be! Believe you can do it! You can!

"When you're at the end of your rope, all you have to do is make one foot move out in front of the other. Just take the next step. That's all there is to it."

—Samuel Fuller and Milton Sperling

125

Useful questions:

- ❖ What can I do today to move me toward my goals?

- ❖ What information do I need to know to begin?

- ❖ How much do I want this, and what am I willing to do to change?

- ❖ What is my first step to do to take action now?

Notes

"Every journey begins with one step."

—Ancient Chinese Wisdom

Blue Moon Wonders and Heart Fire Press are dedicated to publishing books, cassettes, videos and CDs, as well as facilitating workshops to improve the understanding of ourselves and others, and give tools for making positive changes that will enable everyone to create the lives we are all here to manifest.

Feel free to contact us at:
John Seeley at Heart Fire Press
4630 Border Village Road Suite 283
San Diego, CA 92173
www.johnseeleyma.com
949-645-5100

#1 Best-selling Author, International Motivational Speaker, Radio Host and Life Coach, John Seeley has been called Dr. Phil with Soul, He is a much sought after speaker, with a following in 44 countries around the world. He has hosted his own radio shows for more than 10 years, and been featured in the NY Times, The L.A. Times, Woman's World Magazine, The Hong Kong Trader, and numerous other periodicals and on radio and T.V. shows throughout North America.

John grew up the youngest of five children in the Midwest. He lived a normal life until John found his best friend after his friend committed suicide. His life became a roller coaster and finally after many years of searching and study, he discovered how to rebuild his life. Now he helps others to rebuild theirs with grace a lot less struggle than he had.

John holds an undergraduate degree in Business and a master's degree in psychology, and is the No.1 best – selling author of Get Unstuck! The Simple Guide to Restart Your Life, Get Unstuck for Kids! A Fun, Interactive Guide to Empower Your Child for Life, Keep On Believing, Stories of Inspiration, Courage and Triumph, and his latest book Second Chances, Turning Trauma into Triumph, along with other books and articles.

For more information go to www.johnseeleyma.com
Also Check Out www.heartfirepress.com

John uses interactive processes to help people to see things from a different perspective and have hope that they can change their lives and make different choices to create a life of joy.

Available for Keynotes Speaking, Coaching
http://www.johnseeleyma.com